© Aladdin Books Ltd 1990

Design	David West
	Children's Book Design
Editor	Steve Parker
Photo researcher	Cecilia Weston-Baker
Consultant	Neil Harris

First published in the United States in 1990 by Franklin Watts 387 Park Avenue South New York NY 10016

The publishers would like to acknowledge that the photographs reproduced within this book have been posed by models or have been obtained from photographic agencies

Printed in Belgium

Library of Congress Cataloging-in-Publication Data
Randall, Denise Justus.
    Drugs and organized crime / Denise Randall.
        p. cm. -- (Understanding drugs)
    Summary: Discusses the link between organized crime and the drug traffic and also the acts of violence frequently associated with drugs.
    ISBN 0-531-10933-X
    1. Drug abuse--Juvenile literature. 2. Organized crime--Juvenile literature. 3. Drug traffic--Juvenile literature. [1. Drug abuse and crime. 2. Drug traffic. I. Title. II. Series.
HV5801.R28 1990
364.1'77--dc20   89-70582 CIP AC

Contents

UNDERSTANDING DRUGS

DRUGS AND ORGANIZED CRIME

Denise Randall

FRANKLIN WATTS
New York · London · Toronto · Sydney

INTRODUCTION

In most countries of the world, drugs such as heroin, cocaine and marijuana are illegal for people to manufacture, possess and use. The only exceptions the law makes are for medical researchers, doctors and pharmacists.

Governments and courts throughout the world have made these drugs illegal. There are armies of government agents responsible for enforcing laws against the manufacturing, smuggling, trafficking and selling of these drugs. Yet, at the present time there is a serious worldwide illegal drug problem.

The way these drugs destroy people, families and large segments of society is obvious. All you need to do is read a newspaper on any day of the week to learn about drugs and crime. Why are we having so much difficulty stamping out this illegal business?

The illegal drugs business is very organized. In some countries it is as organized as the government itself, and almost as large. It employs hundreds of thousands of people. Blackmail, kidnapping, rape, prostitution and murder are the tools of the leaders of organized drugs crime.

This book takes a long look at the people and events in the world of drugs and organized crime. It explains the links between the leader of a drug empire and someone you might know in your street, school or workplace, who sells drugs or

Shining Path terrorists are said to protect the cocaine trade in Peru.

buys them. They are all in the same illegal and destructive "business."

> ❝ *Effective interdiction must involve enforcement directed against particular criminal organizations and individuals – over and above necessary seizures of smuggled drugs.* **US National Drug Control Strategy, The White House, 1989.** ❞

THE ORIGINS OF ILLEGAL DRUGS

❝ A disease from which no country seems immune...❞

Some illegal drugs come from the leaves or flowers of a variety of plants. Examples are heroin from the opium poppy, cocaine from coca leaves, and marijuana (cannabis) from the cannabis bush. Certain mushrooms and cacti contain substances that cause people to hallucinate, or see illusions which are uncommon in reality. Other drugs are produced entirely by chemical processes, in the laboratory. These include amphetamines and hallucinogens.

❝ Drug abuse is a disease from which no country and no section of modern society seems immune. Former British Home Secretary. ❞

Marijuana

The cannabis plant grows in tropical and subtropical areas. Its natural habitats are Central and South America, the southwestern areas of North America, North Africa, and across southern Asia. It is illegally cultivated in Mexico, Panama, Colombia, the Southwestern United States, Kenya, Morocco, Lebanon, Afghanistan, Pakistan, India, Nepal, Thailand and Vietnam.

Hashish, the concentrated resin of the cannabis plant, is a much more powerful source of the drug. The name, hashish, comes from the Hashishan people of the Middle East who used the drug in religious rituals to prepare themselves for their work – as professional assassins.

Opium poppies are used to manufacture the drug heroin.

Cannabis can be treated in a variety of ways to produce the drug in several different forms. The sap, oil and pollen of the plant can be concentrated into blocks of hashish and smoked. The oil in the hashish can be removed and concentrated to make an even more powerful version of the drug, called hash oil. These simple processes do not require much special knowledge.

Heroin

The opium poppy is the source of heroin. Opium is extracted from the flower and converted into heroin by a chemical process. There are two areas of the world known for growing opium poppies: the Golden Triangle and the Golden Crescent. The Golden Triangle is in Southeast Asia and includes Burma, Laos and Thailand. The Golden Crescent is in Southwest Asia and includes Afghanistan, Pakistan, Iran and Turkey.

Cocaine

Cocaine is extracted from the leaves of the coca plant. The world's center of cocaine production today is in Colombia and Bolivia. Coca was originally grown in Peru for the purpose of chewing coca leaves as a stimulant and for religious rituals.

Manufactured or synthetic drugs

Some drugs are completely man-made using chemical

Leaves of the coca plant are harvested in Colombia.

processes that usually require skilled chemists and sophisticated equipment. These drugs are generally made in the country where they will be marketed. The inner recesses of every major city hides laboratories that are referred to as "drug factories." Four of the best known drugs that come from this source are LSD (lysergic acid diethylamide), amphetamines, crack and ice, as described in the next chapter.

Colourless lives are temporarily heightened by the passing dreamland visions afforded them by the baneful poppy. **Dr. Rayleigh Viccars, 1850.**

PRODUCTION OF ILLEGAL DRUGS

❝ Crack has dominated media attention... ❞

Drug factories

The type and size of drug factories vary from country to country and from city to city. In the United States and Europe, most of these laboratories are small and well concealed in the inner cities. In Colombia and Bolivia, cocaine factories can be much larger and are usually hidden deep in the jungle. They often have an air strip for delivery planes to arrive and pick up a shipment. These factories may produce large quantities of cocaine for a particular country or city.

Pg 30 33

Crack has dominated media attention during the recent surge in drug coverage. **US weekly magazine report.**

Increasing profit by adding fillers

When a drug is first produced it is in its highest state of purity. However, this is not the way the drug reaches the user on the street. Drug producers want to make the highest possible profit, so they "cut" the drug, which means they add "fillers" or "bulking agents" to double or triple its volume. This can double or triple the amount of money they would otherwise make by selling the pure drug. Drug wholesalers who receive deliveries from factories do not sell the drug as they receive it. They also "cut" the drug to increase their profits, adding flour, lactose, or talc. Drug dealers, the "retailers" of the drug world, usually carry out the same process of diluting the drug. The highly diluted form of the drug is sold as the drug by name, but it actually contains a very small amount of the real drug. This is not as effective for the user, since it has been diluted so many times. To the dealers selling the drug to addicts, this simply means more profit, since the addicts will have to buy more of the diluted drug, more often, to achieve the desired effect.

LSD and amphetamines

These are two of the most significant synthetic drugs. They can be produced anywhere in the world. In England, during the late 1980s, the police had great success in finding illicit amphetamine laboratories. They succeeded in destroying 40 of them, which they detected by monitoring the import of certain chemicals into the country. Attempts have been

Cocaine factories use airstrips hidden deep in the jungle.

made to monitor the chemicals used for the manufacture of amphetamines in the United States. However, because the individual chemicals used are often commonly available for legal purposes, it is difficult to use this system as a means of tracing the criminals.

The manufacture of illegal amphetamines has increased in the United States, especially in California. Although manufacture of the drug does take some skill, very common chemicals are used to make it. Some of these chemicals are extremely flammable. There have been instances in which a secret drug laboratory has exploded and set fire to a building.

One of the major centers for the manufacture of "speed," another name for the stimulant amphetamine, is San Francisco. It is thought that the increased interest in amphetamine was in part caused by its use to treat heroin addiction.

The development of new drugs

Most drugs can be used in a variety of ways. Both heroin and cocaine can be sniffed (snorted) or injected. Heroin is not usually sniffed but injected, while cocaine is sniffed since it is not as effective when it is injected.

The enormous sums of money from making and selling illegal drugs are the reason why chemists who work in the drug market are always experimenting with new forms of illegal drugs.

A "cocaine kitchen" equipped for the manufacture of cocaine.

Crack cocaine

Cocaine can be treated with other chemicals and smoked. This is called "freebasing." Cocaine can also be treated in a similar way to produce crack cocaine, or crack.

When the drug market was flooded with cocaine, the availability of the drug encouraged people to think of new ways to sell it. Research chemists working for the illegal drug market were asked by the leaders to create a new type of cocaine. It had to be cheaper and use less of the expensive drug. Yet it had to be stronger and give takers a very powerful "fix" every time they used it. This would make the quantity of cocaine produced in the drug factories go further. It would also give the user a very powerful dose of the drug, for a very short time. When a drug is more powerful, it is also more addictive.

Crack satisfied the search for such an inexpensive and highly profitable, addictive drug. It is made from cocaine by a chemical conversion process that produces hard little crack "rocks" out of the cocaine powder. Cocaine is very expensive; crack is less so. A drug dealer can make more money by selling crack than by selling cocaine because a large amount of crack can be made from a small amount of cocaine. Even though the drug is extremely destructive to the people who use it, the volume of crack being sold keeps going up. It is cheap to buy. It is smoked in a pipe – no needles are required for injecting it.

In many cities in the United States, crack laboratories manufacture thousands of doses of this deadly drug. At first, in 1985, the major cities for production were New York,

Miami and Los Angeles. In 1986, the manufacture of crack was discovered in smaller cities and even small towns throughout the United States.

Crack laboratories are armed fortresses. On the Milton Court housing development in South London, England, police discovered a crack laboratory that was heavily fortified with steel doors. Oxyacetylene torches and a hydraulic ram were needed to break down the door. The people who make and sell crack are not only armed to fight police – they are always ready to fight rival gangs. A US Congressional Committee on Drug Abuse has shown that the amount of money being drained from people addicted to crack is larger than anyone ever expected: $230 billion!

Police officers complete a drugs arrest in Miami, Florida.

Ice

Another example of this search for new ways to sell a drug is "ice." It is made by turning methamphetamine – a powerful amphetamine-type stimulant – into a smokeable form. This drug was developed in Asia and has spread via Hawaii and California to the mainland United States and to Europe.

Ice is highly profitable because the drug producers use less of the pure drug to make it. It is also highly addictive. The effects of smoking it can last as long as 24 hours. But the drug makes its users very violent and causes them to slur their speech, and seem as though they have a mental illness. This last effect is so powerful that it may be difficult for doctors to tell the difference between someone who is using ice and a person who actually is mentally ill.

False prescriptions

One of the medical treatments for heroin addiction is gradually to replace this illegal drug with a legal one, methadone. This can only be obtained from a pharmacy, drug treatment center or hospital dispensary with a prescription from a doctor. It is now known that some dealers go to a drug clinic or a doctor and claim they are heroin addicts. In this way they receive prescriptions for methadone. They do this with several different doctors in different neighborhoods, and go to several hospitals and pharmacies to have the prescription filled. After they receive the methadone, they sell it to heroin addicts.

THE ORGANIZED CRIMINALS

❝They always referred to 'The Mob'...❞

The growth in illegal drugs and organized crime is connected to the vast amounts of money to be made. Many criminals have turned from other forms of crime to the drug market, because profits are high. Because of these enormous amounts of money, the drug business is highly organized.

> ❝ *Europe's switch to cocaine ... is part of a deliberate marketing strategy by South American producers and traffickers.* **Serge Saborin, drug chief at Interpol, in 1988.** ❞

What is "organized crime"?

Organized crime is more than a few people working together to make drugs or smuggle them into a country. It is a network of leaders with large sums of money, who employ dozens of associates, who are responsible for growing, harvesting, manufacturing, packing, shipping and selling illegal drugs. They form a "management" that controls hundreds of people working for them, who carry out all these tasks.

These hundreds of people responsible for the large-scale sale of illegal drugs in turn have thousands of other people working for them, who distribute and sell the drugs. Tens of thousands of street drug dealers sell to hundreds of thousands of drug users. Over time the dealers create more dealers since this is the easiest way to keep a steady supply of illegal drugs moving.

Organized crime has a structure similar to that of a major corporation. But one important difference is that the rule of the leaders is absolute. Mistakes such as revealing informa-tion to the authorities, or stealing a shipment and selling it secretly, are punishable by more than being fired. These errors can carry a death sentence.

The reason it is so difficult to break up the empires of organized crime is because there are so many levels of people between the dealer on the street and the drug "barons" at the top. If any people below the level of leaders are killed or captured, by the authorities or rival empires, they can be easily replaced.

❝ *They always referred to 'The Mob,' or 'The Or-ganization,' or 'The Chiefs.' We didn't know who they really were.* **Former drug pusher, London.**

The cocaine drugs empire

The coca plant is cultivated over large areas of Colombia and Bolivia. The two centers of the drug trade in Colombia are the cities of Medellín and Cali. Each has a drug cartel that controls and operates an illegal drug empire. It is estimated that the wealth of only two of the barons in the Medellín cartel is equal to, or exceeds, that of any top millionaires in the world. Since all profits are illegal and outside the tax system, there are no taxes on them. This makes it even more attractive to criminals.

The huge fortunes controlled by the drug barons give them enormous power over the lives of the people who work for them. Their investment of dollars, risk, intimidation, and murder gives the cartels enormous power. They can

influence the government of their country in their favor through bribes, extortion and assassination.

> 💬 *Their power was everywhere.* **Miami drug trafficker.** 💬

The hold over the farmers

The governments of Colombia and Bolivia want to stop the drug rackets in their countries. The problem is very difficult to solve. There is constant opposition – often violent – to the attempts to fight the drug empires. When the peasant farmers of these countries are offered money just for growing the special crops for drug manufacture, the drug barons increase their power over the farmers. The barons use intimidation, such as beatings, murder, and burning down houses, to keep the farmers growing coca plants.

After coca is planted in a large field, it takes 18 months to produce a first crop. Once this crop is ripe, the mature plants can be harvested four times each year. The lifetime of a healthy coca plant can be as much as 30 years. This means the planting of only two large fields, one after the other, can provide crops for a farmer's lifetime of 60 years.

Cocaine and corruption

The cocaine barons have enough wealth and power to pay government officials and less important employees to slow down the fight against drugs. For example, a shipment of

Weapons seized during a raid on the home of drug baron Pablo Escobar.

bulletproof vests was sent to the Ministry of Justice in Colombia by the United States. The vests were to protect judges from assassination. The Ministry of Justice never received the shipment. It was intercepted by the Ministry of Defense, and the vests were never seen again.

> **It brings together ruthless, hardened criminals and weak, self-indulgent users...** Former British Home secretary.

The cartel's operating structure

At the top of each drug cartel are the drug barons, who are organized into large cooperative efforts called cartels. The cartels grow the coca plants. When the plants are harvested they are sent to laboratories where the leaves are processed to produce cocaine. This is a complicated procedure that has its own underground network for the supplies of specialized laboratory equipment and chemicals. It is all done in secret, and it is highly illegal.

The drug barons have to hide their operations because the government of Colombia is cracking down on the drug trade. When their hideaways are discovered, the cocaine is seized and burned, and the equipment and laboratory are destroyed.

Because they have so much money, the drug cartels can hire armies of people to work for them. Cartels are similar to any major corporation in their size and organization. The

Colombian soldiers search a drug baron's hideaway.

main difference is the lack of fairness and humanity in the way a cartel is run. The barons build their wealth through armies of private soldiers, guards, thugs and petty criminals. They give little to the peasant farmers.

> 💬 *The mob's power was ultimate. They were the control.* **Former drug dealer, Chicago.** 💬

HOW DRUGS REACH THEIR DESTINATIONS

❝ They knew from my friend I'd done some courier work... ❞

The drug trade is a pyramid-shaped empire that has an upper half and a lower half, in two different places. The upper half, down to the packagers, is in the country where the drug is cultivated and processed. The lower half, responsible for distribution, sale and use, is in the country of destination.

It is very difficult to trace a shipment of drugs from its origin to the user. From the arid lands of the Near East to cities in the United States, and from the jungles of South America to the back streets of Europe, a shipment of drugs follows a journey with many twists and turns.

Movements between continents

To get a shipment of drugs from one continent to another may require crossing oceans, when the drugs are carried by plane or by ship. Planes are smaller than ships and cannot carry as much weight, but they can land on remote private airstrips and protect their secret cargos. It is not possible, however, for a small plane to cross the Atlantic or Pacific Ocean with a large shipment.

Planes suspected of carrying drugs can be immediately searched when they land. In this situation, the drugs are usually carried by people called couriers.

Couriers

The amount of a drug a courier can carry is usually very small, but if it is still in its pure form, it is very valuable. The

Drugs in many guises: a haul concealed as sweets.

most important method of smuggling drugs into many cities of the United States and Europe is through the use of couriers. There are ingenious methods of concealing drugs, which include swallowing them. The drugs are sealed in plastic packets which the courier swallows one by one. When the courier arrives at his or her destination, all that is needed to make a delivery is to go to the toilet.

There have been many instances when customs agents have taken X rays of the bodies of suspected couriers, to detect drugs inside. Also, a special toilet has been set up by United States officials that has a clear seat and reservoir. When the toilet is flushed, the contents are sent into a washing chamber, and any packets of drugs can be detected.

Some couriers are professional drug smugglers, who make a living from their business. They regularly risk imprisonment by carrying drugs from one country to another. Other couriers are ordinary people attracted by the lure of earning big money from the occasional drug-smuggling run.

Most couriers have a very limited idea of the chain of events that occurs before they receive the drug and after they deliver it. The courier is only a small part of an extensive network stretching from one continent to another. A courier is usually not told where the drugs are going to, once they are handed over to the next contact. In one drugs trial in London, it was suggested that there were links between the Mafia (see page 36) and the IRA (Irish Republican Army) of Northern Ireland. An American, David Medin, was a drugs courier who carried cocaine. He believed that the IRA had arranged his smuggling trip in Glasgow.

Ships

Large quantities of a drug arriving in a country are most likely to be the result of a ship's cargo. One of the advantages of this method is that a large ship can drop anchor just off the coastline of a country. Smaller boats can then take the drugs ashore along parts of the coast that are not heavily guarded.

Drugs shipped from the Near East, the Far East and Hawaii may be delivered along the Californian coast. Shipments from the Caribbean Islands and South America can be transferred to small boats along the Florida coast.

A drug trafficker is apprehended in the TV series Miami Vice.

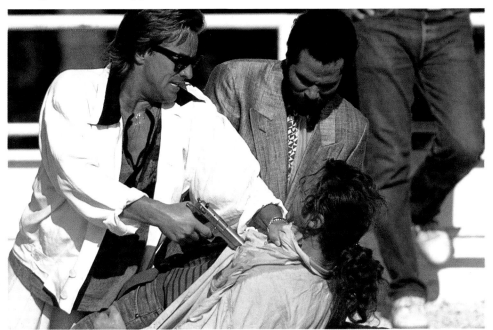

Shipments from South America to Western Europe can enter through the coasts of Spain, Portugal, and Morocco in North Africa. Early in 1989, the police in west Wales, in the west of Britain, raided a number of homes where they seized $3 million in hashish. The drug had been unloaded from a 35-foot boat, the *Rough Diamond*, in a quiet bay.

In countries with a long coastline, the use of boats to smuggle drugs is made easier by avoiding major harbors. Instead of having to dock at a harbor and be searched by customs agents and local police, the drugs are brought to less populated areas where they are secretly transferred to the land. On a long coastline, a boat going to shore is a common sight that does not draw suspicion.

❝ *Most of the cocaine smuggled into Spain, say US experts, is in transit to other European countries...* **Report in** *Time* **magazine.** **❞**

International gangs

There are many legal international corporations that do business in many different countries. The drugs business operates in much the same way, but illegally. The movement of drugs throughout the world has been connected with a variety of international criminal organizations that establish offices wherever they go, hidden in major cities and towns. Some gangs are involved in other illegal activities, besides drug production and trafficking. Other gangs are only

Armed opium warriors of the Golden Triangle in Southeast Asia.

involved in illegal drugs. The Colombian drug cartels operate mainly in Europe and the United States. Couriers sent by the cartels, carrying small volumes of highly purified cocaine, are regularly arrested. For each one caught, it is thought that 10 or more get through.

The Mafia, or Cosa Nostra, is another international crime organization. It became involved in the drug trade shortly after World War II. Another organization is the Triad Gangs which are Chinese in origin. The opium trade is very ancient in China, going back thousands of years. Much of the opium that enters the United States and Europe from the Far East is imported by the Triad Gangs.

Yet another gang is known as the Yardies, from Jamaica. It is very powerful in the cocaine market in the United States, especially in New York and Miami. In Britain, the influence of this gang has been discovered in London, Birmingham, Manchester and Liverpool.

❝ *I was approached in a bar. They knew from my friend I'd done some courier work. But that was 10 years ago.* **Frenchman traveling in South America.** **❞**

Undercover agents

One of the few ways that law enforcement organizations have been able to stop the drug trade is by infiltrating the drug traffickers. Law officers have become dealers, to learn about the people in charge, and they then provide information that leads to the arrest of the criminals. This is done by agencies such as the local police, the Drug Enforcement Administration (DEA) and Federal Bureau of Investigation (FBI) in the United States, and the National Drugs Intelligence Unit in Britain. These agencies maintain relationships with agencies in other countries, to keep track of organized crime and drug trafficking throughout the world.

In Britain, to improve police intelligence from other countries, the National Drugs Intelligence Unit has posted two officers to The Hague, one to Washington DC and another to Madrid.

 We decided to let the shipment go on its way and track the whole gang. **Customs Official.**

Money laundering

Huge amounts of money suddenly being transferred around the world or being spent by any person or organization soon draws suspicion, unless it can be shown that the money comes from a legal business. Money "laundering" is the name given to the way drug profits are hidden. The idea is to find a way to make the money look as if it came from a legal business, when it has actually been generated by crime. The "dirty" money is made "clean" by certain business dealings. This can only be accomplished with the cooperation of financial institutions. Sometimes, banks and accountants and attorneys are unaware that they are helping criminals to stash away or launder their money. At other times, corrupt people take bribes to make the money appear legal.

This does not always work. In Switzerland, a Zurich court

helped legal authorities confiscate more than $12 million deposited by Jose Gonzalo Rodríguez Gacha. He is one of the three Medellín cartel heads who is wanted by the United States government for drug trafficking.

Police in Europe and the United States have the authority to investigate bank accounts that are suspected to be the result of drug trafficking. The police have the authority to trace, freeze and confiscate the profits that come from illegal drug sales.

In Britain, police have been able to examine bank accounts where they suspect there are unaccounted proceeds of drug trafficking under the Drug Trafficking Offenses Act of 1986. Estimates place the drug profits in Britain at an amazing $3 billion.

Drug smuggling and terrorism

The high profit nature of drug smuggling makes it a favorite method of raising money for other criminal activities. Terrorism has been linked to the smuggling and sale of drugs. The money received for the drugs is then used to buy guns and explosives. The sale of drugs involves less personal risk than other methods, such as robbing banks.

In the Middle East, a notorious area for terrorism, the Beka'a valley in Lebanon is a known drug center. Various terrorist groups, including members of Abu Nidal, deal in drugs from their headquarters there. They use the proceeds to finance their other activities. It is suspected that there are

An action-packed drugs raid from the TV series Miami Vice.

heroin laboratories in Lebanon.

Terrorism by its very nature tends to be international in scope. In December 1989, an explosion in Bogotá, Colombia's capital, occurred outside DAS, the country's security and national intelligence agency. Sixty-two people were killed and hundreds injured. DAS have evidence that a member of ETA, the Basque separatist organization from northern Spain, was responsible. ETA is a terrorist organization which has used bombing as a method of bringing itself into prominence. It appears that the drug cartels have made contact with ETA to use its expertise in bombing.

> 〞 *A new heroin and cannabis conduit from the Golden Triangle to Britain has been forged by London criminals.* **News report on the 1989-90 bumper harvest of poppies in Burma, Thailand and Laos.** 〞

DISTRIBUTION – THE ROUTE TO THE CONSUMER

❝ I soon became a dealer... ❞

If you know anyone who is selling drugs – even if he or she is your good friend – that person is the last link in a long chain of events that traces back to the leaders of drug empires. Each link in this chain is a person who is involved in serious illegal activities. As the links in the chain get closer to the drug "barons" or "lords," the leaders, the violence increases. Imagine a person who would think nothing of killing you if you disobeyed his or her orders. This is the person your friend is doing business with if he or she sells drugs. When your friend sells drugs, and if you buy drugs, you are ensuring the survival of people who are controlled by the drug lords. These are the people who rob families, mug, steal and injure. You are also maintaining the drug addicts who might choose you as their next target. The people who buy drugs and use them keep the drug leaders across the world in command of their empires.

Storage and distribution network

Once drugs reach their country of destination, they must be distributed to the wholesaler.

Wholesalers take the large quantities of illegal drugs, repackage them into smaller quantities, and sell these smaller quantities to retailers. The retailers are the dealers on the street who sell the drugs to users.

A drug wholesaler may have a network of storage places where he or she keeps drugs, and places where the drugs are "cut" to make them go further and to generate more profit. Such places may also be used for other purposes, such as a legal manufacturing business or shop, so that other people do not become suspicious.

This part of the drugs business is also controlled by the international gangs of organized crime, from the biggest wholesaler down to the dealer on the street. The distribution business also makes profits and is very valuable. Rival gangs do anything to hold on to their markets.

The war for distribution: gang violence

International and local gangs work together to distribute drugs to wholesalers and dealers. They deal not only in drugs, but also in violence. In the United States, gangs selling crack and gangs selling cocaine have become rivals. Crack is far cheaper – one vial of it sells for about $5.00,

Airport security officers screen baggage for illegal drugs.

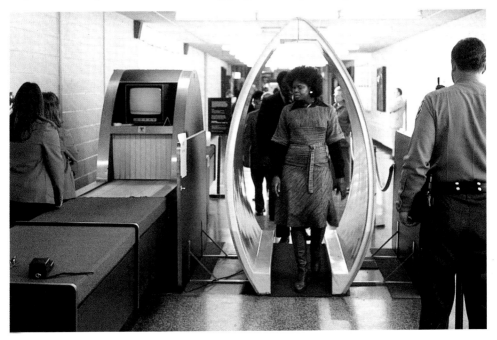

while one gram of cocaine, which looks like about half the amount in a sugar packet, sells for about $100.00. The cocaine dealers and crack dealers sometimes have open shootouts over the control of territory. Not only gang members, but innocent bystanders have been killed during these wars. Very often, a gang offers crack at a reduced price to get people in a neighborhood addicted. Once this happens, they raise the price.

Some parts of cities in the United States, such as New York, are ravaged by organized crime. Gangs fight with their rivals openly in the streets. Many poor communities are dominated by these gangs. Gunfire is a common nightly sound in several New York City neighborhoods and parks. In London, in poorer neighborhoods, drug dealers openly congregate and attract drug users and street corner deals. This has brought normal life to a standstill. The need for drugs has put an end to the growth of a stable society. Daily gang war creates fear and intimidation in a neighborhood. These wars are encouraged by the international criminal organizations. It is organized crime that reaps the profits as people, families, businesses, property and community life are destroyed.

 I thought I would just be an occasional user. I soon became a dealer. **Scottish addict.**

Wholesalers and dealers

Drug distribution by wholesalers to dealers can be structured in a number of different ways. Any or all of them may be used by the international gangs involved in organized crime.

One common method of distribution is a legal business that also has an illegal side. Another is when criminals already engaged in one type of crime, such as robbery, become involved in drug distribution as an offshoot from their regular business.

Sometimes distribution is carried out by hiring different people to carry out individual steps. No one person is aware of the complete route. Distribution can also be carried out by individuals or small groups on an irregular basis. And there are also groups of user-dealers who maintain contact with one another for the purpose of exchanging or selling drugs.

⁇ It is not possible to make a firm distinction between pushers and users. British Policy Studies Institute. **⁇**

Street level distribution

After the dealer buys a quantity of the drug from a wholesaler, he or she will "cut" the drug again, to make it go further. Dealers have to be able to supply users with a steady supply if they want to stay in business.

Once the dealer has established a regular group of users, he or she will try to increase the size of that group by introducing more people to the drug. This increases the dealer's income.

Some dealers are users themselves and only do a small amount of dealing so that they can afford their own drug habit. In Britain the street value of drugs in 1988 was 60 percent higher than in 1987. Yet drug seizures and arrests were only slightly up on previous years.

The large-scale organized gangs often put pressure on the dealers. Wholesalers refuse to sell the drug to a smaller-time dealer unless he or she buys a certain amount. This way the big-time wholesalers maintain or increase their income as well. This effect works back up the pyramid, so that the drug barons maintain and increase their empires and profits.

❝ *More than half of the drug users interviewed had at some time sold drugs.* **Newspaper report.** ❞

ATTEMPTS TO STOP THE DRUG BUSINESS

❝ The rewards are great if we succeed... ❞

Destroying drug crops in Peru

Many countries in the world grow drug crops, and many people in these countries depend on drug money for their income. In some countries, such as Peru in South America, drug crops are the nation's main income. According to its financial records, Peru is a country on the verge of bankruptcy. The official records state that only $12 million is earned from drug crops. The true figure must be closer to $800 million. The government of Peru has been under attack by a Communist terrorist group known as th Shining Path. The Peruvian army has been sent into remote parts of the country where the terrorists hide. The aim of the government is to make sure the general population does not support these terrorists. However, if the Peruvian people have a little bit of land to raise crops, they grow coca plants, from which they can earn good money. They are not interested in politics. They are interested in growing a crop that gives a better income than food crops alone.

The government of Peru is unstable as a result of the attacks by the Shining Path. Although this country has established an anti-drug mission, it is difficult to carry it out. Every time the government tries to destroy drug crops it is attacked by the terrorists. Specialists from the United States Drug Enforcement Administration have been sent to Peru to help locate and destroy the drug crops.

But the people growing the coca plants hate the advisers, Peruvian soldiers and government – those who want to take

Burning is one means of disposal of seized drugs

away their livelihood. They look to the terrorists of the Shining Path to protect them and their illegal crops. Even though the government is planning to introduce substitute crops, to switch the growers' incomes from illegal to legal crops, it would still mean earning less.

Legal weapons

In Britain the Drug Trafficking Offenses Act of 1986 provided a new approach to the fight against organized crime. Instead of concentrating on drugs it enables the police to start at the opposite end of the drug trafficking situation. Section 24 of the Act makes it an offense to enter into or be concerned in an arrangement whereby another person is helped to retain or control his or her proceeds of drug trafficking, knowing or suspecting that the other person has carried on and benefited from drug trafficking.

❝❝ *The rewards are great if we succeed – and the price of ultimate failure is unthinkable.* **Former British Home Secretary.** ❞❞

During the period since the Act has been operative the financial institutions have given assistance to the police when suspicious movements of money in accounts have taken place. If a court order is obtained then bank records and other material can be made available.

Between January 1987 and May 1989 the courts made confiscation orders in respect of about $17 million. However, it is unlikely that this represents the actual amount received. One of the difficulties of recovering money in this way is that it is usually the subject of complicated financial maneuvering.

International initiatives

The United Nations adopted the convention Illicit Traffic in Narcotic Drugs and Psychotropic Substances, in Vienna in December 1988. This is the first time there has been international agreement on tackling the illegal trade in drugs. The idea is for countries to work together to put an end to drug trafficking and remove the drug traders' profits.

In Western Europe, the Council of Europe has developed a Cooperation Group to combat drug abuse and illicit trafficking in drugs. When it was set up in 1971, it had seven members. Over the years it has grown to 19. This group is the basis for European cooperation on drug issues.

Fighting the Colombian drug cartels

The government of Colombia has been waging a war against the drug cartels of Medellín and Cali. In 1988 the Colombian authorities seized nearly 19 tons of cocaine, smashed 900 laboratories and destroyed 76 small airstrips. But even after all that effort, the flow of cocaine into the United States did not decrease. In fact, it increased.

The attempts of the Colombian government to stop the cocaine trade have come up against the wealth and power of the cocaine cartels. The cartels have declared "total war" against the state. The leaders of the cartels are known as "Los Extraditables" because they are in hiding to escape extradition to the United States, where they are wanted for drug trafficking.

The war against coca crops and the cartels has been going on for years. In the early 1980s the Colombian Minister of Justice, Roderigo Lara Bonilla, pursued the cartels and was winning the battle against them. In 1984 he was assassinated. It is believed the contract for his killing earned the assassins one million dollars. Bonilla's successor, Enrique Perejo Gonzalez, also pursued the cartels. In 1987 he was appointed the Colombian ambassador to Hungary. To show their worldwide power, the cartels ordered his assassination in Hungary. Gonzalez was shot five times in the face, but managed to survive.

1989: President Bush and President Barco of Colombia discuss the drugs war.

In August 1989, the cocaine cartels murdered Luis Carlos Galan, a senator in the Colombian government who was very determined to destroy the cartels.

The president of Colombia, Virgilio Barco, became even more determined to destroy the cartels. The cocaine cartels, through corruption and bribery, did all they could to sabotage his efforts. Their vast wealth was used to buy off government officials and employees. So the government increased its attacks against the cartels.

In November 1989, the Medellín cartels decided they would show the government how dangerous they could be. A jet plane taking off from Medellín airport was blown up, killing all 111 passengers and crew.

Fighting drugs in Panama

General Manuel Noriega, the former dictator of Panama, depended upon the cocaine cartels of South America for his power. Noriega was one of the most powerful drug traffickers in the Western Hemisphere. Any attempts by the people of Panama to elect a democratic government were stopped by his army of thugs called the "Dignity Brigade." During late 1989, the United States offered its assistance to the people of Panama. Free elections took place in October 1989. General Noriega used the army and the Dignity Brigade to overturn the election and publicly beat up the man who won the election, President Guillermo Endara.

In early December 1989, General Noriega announced to the people of Panama that he was not afraid of the United States and other countries that declared war against the

cocaine cartels. President Bush of the United States sent the United States Army to Panama in January 1990. Its mission was to protect the people and government of the United States, to capture General Manuel Noriega and leaders of the drug cartels and bring them to trial in the United States.

General Noriega fled from his mansion in Panama City. He was at first hidden by leaders of the drug cartels. The United States Army pursued him to his hiding place. He then sought refuge in the papal ambassador's house, since it is a tradition that a criminal cannot be pursued into a house of God. Noriega hid in the Vatican Mission in Panama for one week. Then he was warned by the Pope's representative that if he did not give himself up, all the other people would leave the building. This would leave him to the people of Panama, who hated him and his involvement with the drug cartels. Noriega gave himself up and was taken back to the United States for trial.

The war goes on around the world

The mission against General Noriega and the drug empire he represented was successful. However, successes are rare. All over the world, trafficking in cocaine, crack, heroin, marijuana, amphetamines, ice and many other illegal drugs is still going on. As the pressure of drug enforcement authorities increases, so does the violence and terrorism of the drug producers, smugglers and sellers. In the Golden

General Manuel Noriega was arrested in January 1990.

Triangle and the Golden Crescent, government officials who try to stop the drug business are assassinated.

It is true that large quantities of drugs are captured and destroyed by the authorities. In the United States, the largest cocaine bust took place in Las Vegas, Nevada. Sixty tons of cocaine and $12 million in cash were confiscated in October 1989. When the person in charge was questioned, he revealed that over $80 million had been collected by his location. This was only one location in only one city.

In March 1990, British customs officials made their biggest ever heroin bust. They seized a truck carrying over 50 kilos of heroin, with a street value approaching $10 million. The officials were suspicious because the truck's markings showed it came from a known drug-producing part of Turkey. The drug was hidden in the gasoline tank.

Throughout the world, the prison terms and fines for drug trafficking are very strict. In Malaysia, the death penalty applies for some drugs offenses. Yet many people still take the risk of making and selling drugs. It is a worldwide epidemic, and we all need to help in stamping it out for ever.

❝ *It requires cooperation between governments, law enforcement agencies, professionals, schools and families.* British Government Statement on stamping out drug abuse. ❞

Mexico, 1989: another drugs haul is destroyed.

FACTFILE

In the United States, there are severe penalties and punishments for being mixed up with drugs. The following is a summary of the federal trafficking penalties under the US Narcotics Penalties & Enforcement Act of 1986.

Heroin

For possession of between 100 and 999 grams, a jail term of between 5 and 40 years for a first offense, and not less than 10 years for a second or subsequent offense. There is also a fine of not more than $2 million for an individual or not more than $5 million for a group or organization.

For more than 1,000 grams (1 kilo), a jail term of not less than 10 years for a first offense and not less than 20 years for a second or subsequent offense. There is also a fine of not more than $4 million for an individual or not more than $10 million for a group or organization. If death or serious injury has occurred, the jail terms are even more severe.

Cocaine

For between 500 and 4,999 grams, as for up to 999 grams of heroin. For more than 5,000 (5 kilos), as for more than 1,000 grams of heroin.

Cocaine base

For between 5 and 49 grams, as for up to 999 grams of heroin. For more than 50 grams, as for more than 1,000 grams of heroin.

PCP ("Angel dust")

For between 10 and 99 grams (100-999 grams of mixture), as for up to 999 grams of heroin. For more than 100 grams (1 kilo of mixture), as for more than 1,000 grams of heroin.

LSD

For between 1 and 10 grams, as for up to 999 grams of heroin. For more than 10 grams, as for more than 1,000 grams of heroin.

Marijuana

The penalties covering marijuana, hashish and hashish oil depend on the form, purity and quantity of the drug. For example, the penalty for trafficking between 50 and 100 kilos of marijuana for a first offense would be a jail term of not more than 20 years, and a fine of $1 million for an individual or $5 million for a group or organization. If death or serious injury has occurred, the jail term is not less than 20 years.

These penalties also apply to between 1 and 100 kilos of hashish oil, or 100 or more cannabis plants.

For a quantity of less than 50 kilos of marijuana, there is a jail term of not more than 5 years and a fine of not more than $250,000 for an individual or $1 million for a group or organization.

DRUG PROFILES

Marijuana This is obtained from the cannabis plant, grown in many tropical and subtropical regions. The leaves can be dried and smoked. Or the sap, oil and pollen can be concentrated into blocks of hashish.

Marijuana does not have such powerful and addictive effects as other illegal drugs.

Heroin The opium poppy is the source of heroin. Opium is extracted from the flowers and converted into heroin by a chemical process. Opium poppies are grown in the Golden Triangle and the Golden Crescent.

Heroin is smoked, or, more usually, injected. Regular users stand a high chance of becoming addicted.

Cocaine This drug is extracted from the leaves of the coca plant, by a chemical process. The world's center of production is South America. Cocaine is usally snorted (sniffed up the nose), though it can be taken in other ways. It can be addictive, especially for the mind.

Crack This is derivative of cocaine. It is made from cocaine powder and other chemicals, by a process that produces small pale "rocks." These are usually smoked in a pipe or similar implement.

Crack gives a powerful but short-lived "high." It is extremely addictive.

LSD and hallucinogens These are made in the laboratory from certain manufactured chemicals. They are usually taken by mouth, as tablets.

These drugs cause hallucinations. Sometimes the effects are short-lived. At other times there are horrifying "flashbacks."

Ecstasy combines the effects of an hallucinogen and a stimulant. People have died after taking only one dose.

Amphetamines and stimulants These drugs, like LSD, are made in the laboratory. They make the body and mind feel energized, though this rebounds after the drug wears off. They are usually taken as tablets or on edible paper. They can be addictive, for both body and mind.

Ice is a new type of stimulant that is smoked. It looks like lumps of ice (frozen water) and is highly addictive.

SOURCES OF HELP

Various organizations will give confidential advice about drug-related problems, including the legal problems involved with simple possession of a drug. However, for those people who begin to get involved in dealing, stealing and other more serious drug-linked crimes, the situation rapidly becomes more complicated. There are no easy answers.

National hotlines

National Cocaine Hotline
1 (800) C-O-C-A-I-N-E

This is a national toll-free number that provides callers with counseling twenty-four hours a day.

National Institute on Drug Abuse
Treatment Referral
1 (800) 622-H-E-L-P

This hotline is staffed from 9:00am to 3:00am on weekdays and from 12 noon to 3:00am on weekends. Counselors can talk with you, refer you to a drug treatment program, or answer questions about drugs, treatment, health or legal problems.

New York State Division of Substance Abuse
1 (800) 522 5353

This toll-free number reaches counselors who can provide referrals for treatment or legal advice, or over-the-telephone crisis intervention.

National Federation of Parents for Drug Free Youth
1 (800) 554-K-I-D-S

This is not a crisis hotline, but a place to call for drug information. This educational organization provides both parents and kids with informational pamphlets, books and videos.

Self-Help Organizations

Cocaine Anonymous
263A W 19th Street
New York, NY 10011
(212) 496 4266

This is a self-help group modeled on Alcoholics Anonymous. To find a local chapter near you, call the number above.

National Self Help Clearinghouse
33 W 42nd Street
New York, NY 10036
(212) 840 1259

Can provide information on self-help rehabilitation organizations in your area, or put you in touch with one of the twenty-seven state and local self-help clearinghouses around the country.

Drug Treatment and Rehabilitation Programs

There are 8,000 to 10,000 drug treatment programs across the country. These include inpatient (residential) and outpatient facilities, covering a range of services: detoxification, counseling, family intervention, aftercare.

National Association on Drug Abuse
355 Lexington Avenue
New York, NY 10017
(212) 986 1170

Conducts a drug prevention program and offers family counseling.

Helping Youth Decide
National Association of State Boards of Education
PO Box 1176
Alexandria, VA 22313
(703) 684 4000

Write for their free booklet about making informed decisions concerning drugs, alcohol, smoking and other issues. This organization also organizes parent-student workshops and community projects.

Legal Advice

Department of Justice
Drug Enforcement Administration,
Washington D.C. Division
400 6th Street S.W.
Washington,
D.C. 20024